One Degree of Change

How to Succeed Now!

Larry A. Jackson

Breastplate Prayer Publications

One Degree of Change
How to Succeed NOW!

This book was written for the person who understands that there is so much more for them to accomplish but just can't seem to breakthrough.

One of the traps in life is being satisfied with a 211 degree life. This is a very good life and many would characterize it as a successful life. But for the person who should be living at 212 degrees they feel like the oyster with sand in its shell, very agitated. Many times they can't put their finger on what is wrong or what is needed.

Even the Christian living a good life before God can feel that something is missing. The thing missing is their purpose. They love the Lord and all that He provides but they realize there is more they should be doing for Him.

If you feel like you are not walking in your purpose then this is the book for you. *One Degree of Change: How to Succeed Now!* will open your heart and mind to just how close you really are to accomplishing what the Lord has designed you for. It will provide much needed answers for your advancement. **Because you are only one degree from the success you desire.**

A New Attitude

Most people today desire some form of change in their lives even though they may not articulate it. Whether that change is personal, relational, physical, financial, spiritual or something altogether different, it's safe to say that nearly everyone would welcome a metamorphosis that would increase, improve and/or advance their lives in some way.

The self improvement industry capitalized on this increasing wave of discontent by supplying products and programs to assist those aiming to achieve a particular goal. Forbes reported that Americans spent $11 billion in 2008 on self-improvement materials such as books, CDs, seminars, coaching and stress-management. Surely you have seen infomercials that touted its products as being revolutionary and, by making one phone call, your life will change forever! It's just that easy.

To prove this point, another report by Forbes in 2008 indicated that Americans spent $1.4 billion pursuing the American dream described by someone on television. What the viewer fails to understand is that the change they are seeking isn't found in a product or program, even though these tools can be used as a catalyst to help reenergize their ability to dream. The catalyst is seen as the reason for change when what really happens is the person who purchased the product or program believes they can change and begins to dream again. Once they reactivate their imagination and dream center, it becomes much easier to advance in life and to accomplish the things that once appeared to be too difficult or even impossible to achieve.

One of the main reasons why these companies continue to sell so many products is because most people don't realize that the change they desire is already with them each day as they live on this earth. This statement may sound strange and some may even consider it to be hype, especially those who have struggled for years to change or have given up their pursuit altogether.

For this reason, I felt compelled to write a book to help Christians and non-Christians understand that God provided the answers they need in the Bible. If a person can believe and apply the principles contained in this book, the changes they desire can become their reality.

This is not because I think or say so, but because the Word of God declares it! Unlike the self improvement industry whose aim it is to take advantage of people's fears, weaknesses and shortcomings; or strategizes on ways to siphon money out of as many bank accounts as possible. God has already proven that He loves and wants the best for mankind, and He paid it all. As proof of His desire for their well being in every area of life, God provided the solution for every problem that is common to man within His Word.

Consider the following Scripture in which God expresses His desire for the human race:

> **Beloved, I wish above all things**
> **that thou mayest prosper and be in**
> **health, even as thy soul prospereth.**
> *3 John 1:2*

This verse clearly reveals God's heart toward mankind. Therefore, if His genuine desire is for people to prosper and be in health, then He must have provided a plan, principles or both to help people obtain what He promised.

The self improvement industry primarily targets three specific areas; prosperity, health, and knowledge. It should come as no surprise to you that the Bible addresses each of these topics at length. However, it is man's responsibility to diligently search the Scriptures for God's plan for each area and begin to apply what they learn. You will find more about how to actually accomplish this later, but for now, just know that everything you need is in the Bible.

Eureka

For nearly twenty years, I've had the pleasure of being a platform speaker for Promise Keepers (PK), a national men's movement. One of the highlights that precede these events is the speakers' summit, which takes place annually in Denver, CO. Every year, PK convenes the platform team to discuss the upcoming year and how we will approach our individual topics. It is a homecoming of sorts for all of us!

One year while attending the summit, the co-founder of the ministry, Coach Bill McCartney (Coach Mac), spoke to us about our responsibility and the importance of speaking to the thousands of men who would attend a Promise Keepers stadium event that year. He was drawing a parallel between our role as platform speakers and that of a coach preparing his/her players for a big game against their rivals.

Coach Mac was the head football coach at the University of Colorado Boulder from 1982 to 1994. He compiled a record of 93–55–5 and won three consecutive Big Eight Conference titles between 1989 and 1991. Coach Mac's 1990 team was crowned national champions by the Associated Press, splitting the title with Georgia Tech University. Without question,

Coach Mac clearly understood what it took to prepare a team to be the best they can be and to accomplish their goals.

Coach Mac also indicated that the importance of the game had more to do with the preparation and attitude of the team than what was said to them or the plays in the playbook. During a long season, all of the games were important to the overall success of the team, but there were a few games that carried great significance. Even though I have a great love for football, the anecdotes from an accomplished coach about his teams' successes and failures captured my attention. However, I connected with these stories on a completely different level.

Coach Mac's talk to the speaking team resonated greatly with me because I was a starting quarterback in high school. My football playing days were long gone and replaced by family, ministry and a host of other things. Since that time, I hadn't given much thought to the level of focus and excitement that marked the big games we played; that is, not until that afternoon.

As I listened to Coach Mac, I started to reminisce about those days, recalling the emotions that surrounded game day. I weighed the differences between the big games and all of the other games on our schedule. It quickly became apparent that there was very little difference in the preparation time during practice or even the time we spent watching film. The difference was in the *way* we prepared. Allow me to explain.

For the big games, everyone seemed to get more out of the time we had. Even though the overall goal was to win every game, we paid a lot more attention to these. Our attitude changed without anyone having to motivate us with an emotional pep talk; even though we would receive several leading up to the kick off.

The sounds on the field intensified during practices leading up to the big game. We could sense a shift in the atmosphere, a different kind of energy. Excitement filled the air. You could hear it as we ran around the track before practice or when we broke the huddle before running a play. Everyone on the team wanted this game and was willing to work hard to get it. The team was locked in, focused on the task at hand and determined to win.

What I realized as I listened to Coach Mac was that our corporate attitude shift had made the difference. I also understood that for me to change my attitude in any given situation, I had to determine if what I desired was important enough for me to adjust my attitude. This is exactly what made the rival game more important than the other games on the schedule.

Focus on the Principles

Even though this book isn't about sports or sports teams, you will find the underlying principles that set great teams apart throughout. For this reason, I will use several sports related examples to help drive home this one degree principle.

My experiences in sports helped me relate to the examples Coach Mac shared that day about preparing a winning team. Remember, he was speaking to a group of national and international speakers who had signed on to be part of the Promise Keepers team. These men had many years of experience sharing the gospel message, but Coach Mac was helping us to change our mindset from being a speaker at just another meeting to seeing Promise Keepers at an entirely different level.

More than Will Power

It is important that I distinguish between positive thinking and kingdom transformation. Positive thinking is done by sheer will power; to the contrary, the Word of God and a transformed mind bring about kingdom transformation.

As I mentioned earlier there are thousands of books and CDs designed to teach people how to think positively. Not for one second am I suggesting that positive thinking is a bad thing. Believe me; I understand the importance of positive thinking. Encounter someone with a negative attitude and you will understand the importance of being positive as well.

Unlike the training provided in the world, a person can develop a positive attitude by applying the principles outlined in the Word of God. Rather than strengthening the mind, the Bible actually transforms it. The Apostle Paul's letter to the church in Rome exhorted them to do just that.

> **And be not conformed to this world:**
> **but be ye transformed by the**
> **renewing of your mind, that ye may**
> **prove what is that good, and**
> **acceptable, and perfect, will of God.**
> *Romans 12:2*

Paul is saying just because the world is loud doesn't mean its right. Do things God's way; don't follow the course of society.

In 1 Peter 1:13, the Apostle Peter urges us to develop a right attitude and soberness about life.

> **Wherefore gird up the loins of your mind, be sober, and hope to the end for the grace that is to be brought unto you at the revelation of Jesus Christ;** *1 Peter 1:13*

It is so important to understand how God's Word actually transforms the mind for both spiritual and natural advancement. Transforming the mind God's way leads to lasting change that will forever produce the results desired.

I acquired this understanding in the natural during my playing days. The principle worked, but it wasn't lasting for I had not gained a spiritual understanding. The Word of God will transform the mind when we follow its eternal principles.

More Time, Please

Many people today regularly attend church and read their Bibles; yet, few are actively using the Bible to transform their minds and, ultimately, their lives. This is because it takes time and focused effort to accomplish their desired end. With so many demands vying for their attention, there still doesn't seem to be enough time left to work on themselves.

For instance, if you are married, have children, and/or a demanding career, then you can appreciate my last statement. Even single people find it difficult to set time aside for themselves.

For single parents, there are an infinite number of responsibilities involved in meeting the needs of their child/children that make it virtually impossible for them to find time for self improvement projects. Healthy children's websites also address common issues that frequently confront single parents, including being over tasked, children becoming a burden, non-custody parent issues, custody parent issues, reduced time and energy.

The process that consumes our time is commonly known as the *tyranny of the urgent*. I define "urgent" as the issues that scream for attention now. Even though there may be more important matters at hand, far too often, we prioritize the urgent, thereby forcing everything else to take a backseat or even drop off the list completely. It is unfortunate, but this is one of the primary reasons why self-improvement can be difficult or even seem impossible to start or to finish. Let me say, you must be willing and determined to accomplish the impossible!

Make the Adjustment

Since change always begins with a paradigm shift, we can start by thinking differently about time. Time is precious and we must begin to consider it from this viewpoint. When we don't understand the importance of each moment, we fall victim to time robbers throughout the day. They include extensive television watching, excessive amounts of sleep or talking on the phone, social media and even over working. It serves us well to learn to manage or even eliminate these and other activities that steal our time. It is for this reason that a 'things to do' list containing tasks to complete your goals must be prepared for each day.

A New Coach

When I played football, our coach called special practices that completely disrupted our lifestyles and agendas. It didn't matter what we had planned, we were required to attend. Coach had that level of control over our time because we wanted to be part of the team and all that it represented. We also understood that a commitment to winning involved sacrifices.

The time has come for a new coach to take charge and you are that person. If you desire change, you are the one who must oversee and train your soul like a coach oversees and trains the team. Start by resolving to take ownership of and then gain the mastery over any time robbers that persist in your life. Adopt a "whatever it takes" mindset. I will discuss the role of a life coach later in the book, but keep in mind that, even with a life coach, personal coaching must occur regularly in order to continue forward progress.

Getting It Done

Since many people find it easier to follow a plan that is laid out step-by-step, I will use this format to present the plan. I have structured the plan in a way that shouldn't interfere with most people's lives; however, some may require more discipline than others to keep from getting sidetracked by their busy schedules. Remember, you owe it to yourself and to those who will benefit from your commitment to follow through and complete the plan. However, it is very important that you carve out the time to do so.

According to The Choice Driven Life with Olga Herman, here are five qualities of finishers:

1. They are hard-working.
2. They are willing to work in unpleasant and inconvenient circumstances.

3. They are adaptable to changes that will improve their performance.
4. They are proud of what they have done, but aren't so satisfied that they stop prematurely.
5. They persist until they have crossed the finish line!

Accomplishing your desired transformation will require adopting most or all of these qualities.

Instructions Not Suggestions

Recently, I looked at a bottle of supplements on my counter and decided to read the directions. To my surprise, they suggested that I take the pills three times daily. I was only taking them once per day. Consequently, I received some benefit, but not all that I could have received had I followed the directions. Many times in life we receive proper instructions, but fail to follow them. It is imperative that you follow the directions outlined at the end of this book to receive the maximum benefit.

First and foremost, the plan provides a platform for developing a new attitude! It is well documented that attitude is more important than aptitude.

Nothing can stop the man with the right mental attitude from achieving his goal; nothing on earth can help the man with the wrong mental attitude.
Thomas Jefferson

The longer I live, the more I realize the impact of attitude on life. Attitude to me is more important than facts...We cannot change our past...we cannot change the fact that people will act in a certain way. We cannot change the inevitable. The only thing we can do is play on the string we have, and that is our attitude. I am convinced that life is 10 percent what happens to me and 90 percent how I react to it. And so it is with you...we are in charge of our attitudes.
Charles R. Swindoll

Your mental attitude is something you can control outright and you must use self-discipline until you create a Positive Mental Attitude - your mental attitude attracts to you everything that makes you what you are.
Napolean Hill

The optimist sees opportunity in every danger; the pessimist sees danger in every opportunity.
Winston Churchill

There are times when a person still needs guidance and motivation, even when they have the right attitude. That is why a life coach has such a critical role in this plan. A life coach helps a person stay focused when life takes an unexpected turn or when the person becomes content before they've reached their goal. I will go into more detail about the function of the life coach later. However, it is essential that we understand that this is one of the reasons why Jesus commanded His disciples to go disciple the world.

> [18]And Jesus came and spake unto them, saying, All power is given unto me in heaven and in earth.
> [19]Go ye therefore, and teach all nations, baptizing them in the name of the Father, and of the Son, and of the Holy Ghost:
> [20]Teaching them to observe all things whatsoever I have commanded you: and, lo, I am with you alway, even unto the end of the world. Amen.
> *Matthew 28:18-20*

The mentor or coach will help a person get to their desired goal or position in life when they can't seem to get there on their own.

One of the greatest coaches in my life has been Bishop Wellington Boone. Bishop Boone took me as a young Christian and discipled me spiritually as well as naturally into the person I am today. I have always been a self starter and personally motivated. Much of this came from my coaches in my earlier years. My parents also taught me to finish what I started and to finish well. However, it was Bishop Boone who challenged me to go further and accomplish more than I could even imagine. This book is an example of Bishop Boone's leadership and mentoring that strengthened me beyond my comfort zone.

I had never thought about writing a book. In fact, I only read the books necessary to take tests. I very seldom read just for pleasure. Bishop Boone helped me believe that it was possible for me to be an author. Now I have authored 12 books with several in the quarry.

In addition to writing books, I now conduct a class to help others understand how to write their own books. It pleases my heart to know that six of the students I've taught are now authors and there will be many more to come. I credit Bishop Boone for pushing me to do what I didn't think was possible.

A life coach helped me move from 211°F to 212°F in my mindset. I was only one degree away and, if I hadn't moved, then this book and none of the others would be on bookshelves around the world.

Hot But Not Boiling

Let's revisit the speech given at the speakers' summit that inspired this book. As I listened to Coach Mac and looked back on my own playing days, even while considering what Bishop Boone had done for me, I began reflecting on the process water undergoes to reach the boiling point. I realized there is only one degree that separates extremely hot water and water that is boiling. Water that is 211°F will cause a serious burn on a person's body, but water doesn't start boiling until it reaches 212°F; i.e., one degree of change.

> -Quick reference to Water boiling point (Not Steam Temp) at different pressures- The boiling point of water raises 3 degrees F per each pound of square inch pressure added. For example: at sea level, water will boil at 212 degrees F (100 deg C). +1 PSI over sea level it will raise the boiling point 3 degrees F, to 215 degrees F (1.7 deg C, to 101.7 deg C). At +5 PSI over sea level the boiling point of water will be 227 degrees F (108.3 deg C). And so on. This is why directions

for boiling noodles and baking goods at high altitudes require longer cook times, and/or more water added to mixture.

This book is entitled "One Degree of Change" because the change for which most people are looking is closer than they think. In the same way a steam locomotive starts to move once the engine reaches the right temperature, your success will take place once your temperature crosses the threshold.

Many people who have good lives stop short of or even give up on their pursuit of complete freedom and success. Far too often it is because they determine that reaching the desired change is more difficult than they expected.

Remember, the only requirement for water to reach its boiling point is for it to stay connected to a heating source. If a person is willing to stay connected and work smarter and not harder, their potential will increase the same way the temperature of the water increased. Reading books like this one while using research to increase your knowledge are the first steps. Believe me; you are on the right track!

New Energy

Once water reaches its boiling point, it changes from a liquid into steam. This change in energy allows for an infinite number of uses for which water would not be suitable. Steam has a vital part in the manufacturing of over 80 percent of goods made in America. These products include plastic and vinyl components in automobiles, stains and paints we use on our homes, and cleaning products for our bathrooms and kitchens. We use steam to prepare some of the foods we eat and even to remove wrinkles from our clothes.

Earlier in the book, I described the times when, as a team, we collectively adjusted our attitudes and practice habits in order to win the big game against our rival. By doing so, what each of us needed to be more successful on game day fell into place. Even so, what I don't want to do is make the change process sound so simple that it appears automatic or trite. There is work involved, but the process is easier than most realize. Anyone willing to embrace the proper attitude, combined with determination and energy, and take the appropriate actions, will accomplish their goal despite any obstacles they encounter along the way. It will feel like a breakthrough or like water transforming to steam. Everything will become much easier.

To The Victor Goes the Spoils

The big game was always the one that everyone looked forward to playing. This game gave us the opportunity to win the title and bragging rights for an entire year against our conference or cross-town foes.

On a college level, athletic conferences in Divisions 1 and 2 have aligned themselves and scheduled most of the rivalry games on the same weekend. This week is known as "Rivalry Week". Usually a trophy passes between schools, with the victor keeping the trophy until the following year when the teams meet again. This trophy is second only to winning the national title. However, if the team wins the national title, but loses against their rival, the season wasn't complete.

Sport teams understand the difference between hot and boiling. They definitely want to be boiling when they face their big game. Many times the explanation given for a team getting into post season play is that they got hot at the right time. This is just another way of saying their attitudes shifted. "They started to boil!"

Looks Are Deceiving!

For those engaged in the game of life, the big game is the opportunity to live a better life, provide more for their families, leave pain behind and a host of other benefits that a person functioning at a 211°F lifestyle can miss. What makes this so interesting is that living a 211°F lifestyle can be very good. There are many great creature comforts associated with it. Family and friends of those enjoying this type of life may even desire to have a similar lifestyle.

What people don't understand or even consider is how much more the person with the 211°F lifestyle wants or needs from life. Just because everything looks good on the outside doesn't mean that everything is good!

The Game from Another Vantage Point

The rivalry game has many different components. One that I find interesting has to do with the fans. The rival team's fans come to the same stadium, they wear their team's colors and they sometimes sit in relatively close proximity to the other team's fans. The most striking difference between these fans is their mindset about the game. They want their team to win at all costs and they cheer just a little bit louder during the game.

These fans don't want last week's win or even last year's win over the rival. They want victory this year and they are all in to help make it happen. The 211°F cheers worked for the game against the other teams, but they have to turn it up a notch for this game.

The team doesn't want to let the fans down either, so they try just a little more during the game. The announcers will say that the team is feeding off of the fans' emotions and cheers. Sometimes you will see a player asking the fans to cheer even more. Everyone is all in and they all want the same thing; the win!

How does this help us in our quest to see change take place in our lives? Remember the only thing that changed about the rivalry game was the way the players and fans thought about it. How are you thinking about life? Are you thinking about winning, just surviving or are you so low that you are thinking about how not to lose?

Unfortunately, many Christians live this way even with all the Bible has to say about blessings, increase and prosperity. During my travels, I engage many Christian believers who are just trying to survive, but if you listen to them pray or talk, everything appears to be just fine. What I have found is that most people have one image about life and attempt to form another image of how they want their lives to be while in prayer or attending church. Yet the Scriptures clearly state that this mindset will not work because the person praying is double minded.

> **A double minded man is unstable in all his ways.** *James 1:8*

> **Draw nigh to God, and he will draw nigh to you. Cleanse your hands, ye sinners; and purify your hearts, ye double minded.** *James 4:8*

In the same way, players who tells others their team will win, but inwardly they only hope they don't lose usually have no chance of winning because of their double mindedness. This is a true statement about which everyone can agree; the team cannot be double minded about their chances in the game.

There is one thing to note about loyal fans, they believe in their team. They come to the game with the belief and attitude that their team will win no matter the circumstances.

Single Focus

In sports, there is a term called "circling the date" on the schedule. The coaches, players, and fans start thinking about this game during the off season and preseason training. Once the season starts, everyone starts talking about and making plans to attend this game. With everyone focused on the win, the team develops a winning mindset. There is a downside to this; namely, this can also become a distraction, making it difficult for the players to stay focused on the other games.

Many times you will hear a coach or even a player use the phrase "One game at a time". Even though it sounds good, it is not true and everyone knows it. It is an attempt to help the team stay focused and not look ahead to a big game weeks away. Coaches use the term, even though they are looking ahead themselves.

It is not unusual for a team to lose to a lesser opponent, especially when the big game is close at hand. How does this happen? When a team becomes preoccupied with winning a single game, it's very easy to lose sight of the big picture, which is to win every game.

This can also happen in life when we begin focusing on our change, but the issues of life become more urgent than the change we are seeking. Earlier, I introduced the term 'the tyranny of the urgent.' Now allow me to explain why it is important to understand where the urgent matters can often originate and what can happen when we fall into this trap.

Family and Friends (a.k.a. Fans)

Be aware that some of these urgent matters can come from loved ones and friends who want their situation to become someone else's burden. Other people's problems and even progress can impede your ability to change, especially when they create additional tasks and/or responsibilities that could derail your efforts. Most of the time people aren't intentionally trying to be a hindrance. They are looking for help and a way out of a difficult situation. They are blinded to anything that isn't directly helping them at the time. By bringing you into the issue your focus and pursuit is stopped and the problem wasn't even yours. Please believe me. Hell understands how to use others to completely affect what is taking place your life.

Not In a Vacuum

Inform those who need to know that you are in the first stage of a self-improvement process. Tell them that, for the next few months, there will be times you will not be available. Afterwards, things will get back to normal. Should someone want more information, just tell them you will be able to discuss it more once you have completed the process.

Please don't attempt to give information about the process or principle until there is fruit others can examine. Believe me, these people have kept score of your successes and failures and they will want to see evidence before them to show you are changed or successful. You will have an excellent opportunity to give in-depth information about the process once everyone sees that you have achieved your goal. Your victory or change will speak so loudly that those closest to you will want to listen and learn how to do what you have done.

Money or the lack there of, can appear to be an urgent matter in many situations. A person can think about money so much that nothing else matters in their life. Vision produces money but money does not produce vision.

Don't Look Back

Another great aspect of this process is that there is nothing to purchase to get started. Money will never be an obstacle. Most people already have everything they need. In fact, there is no need to even change a person's current routine, work schedule or lifestyle; that is, as long as it is legal and honest. As a side note, a person's conscience will automatically work against any positive change taking place in their life if there is any involvement in dishonest or illegal activity. To move forward, the person must resolve this matter.

It is important to remember that Jesus came to the earth to bring mankind back to their original place with God. The Bible clearly tells us that through His sacrifice, the blood cleanses the conscience of everyone who embraces the finished work of Calvary (Hebrews 10:22). For most people, when their conscience is cleansed, a systematic change must occur in the way they think and the attitudes they embrace. Repentance is a changing of the mind and walking in a new way that indicates the new way of thinking.

Change Your Thoughts

The mind is the greatest computer ever created. It is a composite of everything a person has ever seen, heard, said, felt and done in their lifetime. In fact, the human mind created and built the super computers that we rely on today.

A human being has about 100 billion brain cells. Although different neurons fire at different speeds, as a rough estimate it is reasonable to estimate that a neuron can fire about once every 5 milliseconds, or about 200 times a second.

https://www.ualberta.ca

You've undoubtedly heard over and over again about what an absurdly complex entity the human brain is. But a new breakthrough by Japanese and German scientists might finally drive the point home. Taking advantage of the almost 83,000 processors of one of the world's most powerful supercomputers, the team was able to mimic just one percent of one second's worth of human brain activity—and even that took 40 minutes.

gizodo.com Ashley Feinberg

Oftentimes, the one desiring change and advancement can link the barriers to change to negative words and experiences they have had in life. Loved ones and friends may share unsolicited opinions regarding their aspirations, even proclaiming that what they desire can't be accomplished. Yet, in spite of the opposition, everything inside of the person's heart believes they can achieve their desire, so they set their heart to do it.

Frequently when a person is bombarded with negative comments and opinions it is difficult for the person to develop an accurate picture of their future. Therefore when that person starts to think about how to prepare and take ground necessary for advancement, thoughts planted in their mind by well-meaning people can and, most likely, will surface. Before long, this person's words can begin to align with those negative words spoken by those who don't believe.

Remember, everything we say and do originate in our thoughts, including those imparted by others. Eventually, these thoughts become words, which may lead to actions that can work against the plans and purposes of a person's life.

The Power of Words

When we begin to speak our thoughts, everything around us conforms to what we have spoken. This may seem unusual, but keep in mind that this is the way all of creation came into existence; by the spoken Word.

Words are thoughts given voice and will either cause a person to win with confidence or struggle with a "hope it will work" attitude. Words are thoughts that connect with and expose what is in the heart. The Bible declares that our words come from the heart.

> **O generation of vipers, how can ye, being evil, speak good things? for out of the abundance of the heart the mouth speaketh.** *Matthew 12:34*

Years of hearing "you can't", "you won't", or "you never will be or do" take quite a toll on a person's mind. Negative words and experiences may leave them feeling like a prisoner with chains around their ankles and wrists and tape over their mouth, with little hope of ever being free and the chances for success, slim.

Many times parents will use negativity in an attempt to motivate their child hoping that telling them they won't or can't do something, will cause them to work harder and prove them wrong. What usually happens is they create a bruised ego and a lack of confidence in the child. Then the parent cannot understand why the child who has become an adult can't seem to be successful.

Words Are Important!

If you listen to someone talk about their desire to change, whether it's personal or relating to their circumstances, their words are key to whether their change will occur in the near or distant future. The distance it takes to get from their head to their heart is the determining factor. Whenever we talk, whether to someone else or to ourselves, we are listening at the same time. Even if we don't realize it, our words affect our perception. They give us permission to move forward or to embrace defeat. By learning to control our words, we can keep ourselves focused in the right direction.

Look Forward

Therefore, it is vitally important to use the Bible to cleanse the mind of any experience that will hinder you from achieving your goal. The Word of God helps us stop looking back at our failures and shortcomings; it silences the harsh, critical words spoken by well-meaning or evil people; it uproots lies we've believed and replaces them with truth. As we learn to think differently, we can look toward the future with confidence.

Remember, Lot's wife was told not to look back as she and her family fled from Sodom and Gomorrah's destruction. Unfortunately, she did not heed the angel's warning and was turned into a pillar of salt. The principle works the same when people think back on the adverse circumstances they've gone through. Just thinking about it oftentimes completely immobilizes the person. Learning to think forward thoughts can be a task in itself, but anyone can do it by using the Word of God.

Understanding the Principle

The Bible teaches in Proverbs 23:7, "For as he thinketh in his heart, so is he". This may sound strange since everyone knows the heart doesn't think, or does it? Why would the wisest man who ever lived, other than Jesus Christ, write about a man's heart being able to think if it was not possible? We readily accept that the heart *feels,* since one of the words we use to describe our emotions is *heartfelt*. The heart to which Solomon refers isn't the organ that keeps us alive by supplying blood throughout the body, but rather the soul of man.

The soul consists of the mind, will, and emotions, and can be directly connected to the personality of a person. When you hear phrases such as "the heart of the matter" and "what is in your heart", it is referring to the soul and not the natural heart. As I stated earlier, the soul stores everything we know about ourselves and others and the super software of the soul runs the hardware called the brain.

In Proverbs 23:7, Solomon is trying to help us understand how powerful thinking or meditation can be in our lives. When we meditate on a particular area of life, that area *becomes* what we meditate.

The complete transformation of the soul takes place by using the Word of God. When we do this properly, everything changes. There are some lifelong church members who haven't discovered this about the Bible. Many of them enjoy the benefits of preaching and even reading the Bible, however, as a whole, purposeful transformation has seemed to escape the body of Christ.

What is most fascinating about using the Bible to transform the soul is that it is effective for *anyone* who will use it. This is the goodness of God at work! The Word of God moves a person from 211°F to 212°F without them having to struggle to get there.

Since a person's will power can get them to 211°F, many think they can reach the boiling point through positive thinking or materials such as books and conferences. These tools can only produce a very hot 211°F. We have already acknowledged how a person can be successful and even envied by their loved ones and friends, yet they still feel as though they are lacking in some way.

As I pointed out in Matthew 12:34 earlier the Bible teaches that out of the abundance of the heart the mouth speaks. This is the same heart to which Solomon refers in Proverbs 23. In other words, not only does the heart think, it speaks as well. Therefore, it is in the heart that the one degree of change must take place.

Before we turn our full attention to the area you want to change, let's think about the final preparations before the big game again. The coach will tell the team to get their hearts into the game. Sometimes, he may use the word mind, but that's not often. He will refer to the way the team practiced, how they warmed up; their focus, how they competed, and how that translated to the game. So, what does he see? What are the indicators that will determine if the team will play well during the game? It's heart! He wants to insure that their hearts are actively involved. Their body language will indicate how much corporate focus they have.

I Know, I Hope

All of the practice and pregame preparation helps to build each team's confidence. They enter the game with a mindset and a hope to win. One team is confident and excited, while the other team is trying to show excitement, but they aren't as confident. For the second team, also known as the "underdog" everything has to go well or what they really believe will surface as soon as things start to go against them. "Here we go again" are the underlying thoughts the players don't communicate before the game.

Everything doesn't always go well for the first team, also known as the "favorite", but they keep the mindset that they will still win. This could be due to the trust the players have in their coach to make the necessary adjustments during the game or at halftime. It could also be because of the confidence they have in each other or one of their teammates who, because of his winning attitude, will not allow the others to doubt the outcome.

The underdog team comes into the game with the hope that they can do what they practiced; while the first team enters the game knowing they can accomplish what they practiced. During the game, when the favorite doesn't play to their potential, I've heard the announcers say, "They are giving the second team hope." In this case, the underdog begins to think they can actually win the game. We use the term "momentum shift" to indicate that things have started turning to the benefit of the underdog. If the shift continues, the team that came in as the underdog leaves the game as the winner.

What happened?!

The underdog experienced an attitude shift, which provided the energy they needed to make the extra play, run faster, and make believers out of their fans. It all took place at the same time.

Now, what about you?

What represents the big game in your life? Please, don't get me wrong. I am well aware of the fact that life is not a game. But, in keeping with (in light of, in line with) the sports theme, stories, examples, and my experiences cited thus far what is your challenge? There may be several undertakings you'd like to achieve, but which one will cause all of the dominos in your life to fall into place? This is the one upon which you should focus all of your attention and energy.

Even though all of us use our minds continuously throughout the day, many today have underdeveloped concentration skills. We have been trained (mesmerized) by the media to take mental breaks through endless television commercials. Without being aware of this, our minds take mini-vacations at times when it should be alert. Many times, because we are so easily distracted, we completely forget about that upon which we should be focused, so we turn our attention to something new.

All photographers and camera operators understand that to get high-quality photos, one of the things they must do is to focus the lens of their cameras. Our lives are no different. We need a clear picture of what we want to accomplish and that takes focus. Can you imagine how the photos would look if the photographer allowed dust, fingerprints or other particles to soil the lens? Or how many of us have tried to take a picture only to realize the lens cap was still on? Both of these examples illustrate how some think about life and their ability to succeed.

When you think about the goals in your life, assuming you have goals, what words come to mind? Are they words like I hope, maybe someday or I just need a break? If so, then your lens is dirty. But if you don't have any goals and objectives, then your lens cap is covering your lens.

In his book *What They Don't Teach You at Harvard Business School*, Mark H. McCormack cited a study conducted in 1979 on new graduates from the Harvard MBA Program. When asked if they had clear, written goals with plans to accomplish them, three percent had written goals and plans, 13 percent had goals, but they were not committed to paper and 84 percent had no specific goals at all. When conducting a second interview with these graduates ten years later, the three percent who had clear, written goals made ten times as much as the other 97 percent *combined*. Their success was directly attributed to the execution of the goals they set.

But one thing that could be overlooked is the fact that each graduate had their goals written with target dates. Setting goals helps with focus.

Talking Loud; Producing Nothing

Nowadays, people know the right words to say, but many don't really believe their own words. Not having clear goals and plans, the lack of focus and sometimes fear itself may explain why some inwardly struggle with doubts. This is characteristic of the underdog mindset described earlier.

Remember in the two teams example I mentioned an instance of when the announcer at the big game would say the team seen as the favorite to win wasn't playing to their potential. Well, I have some bad news for you. Unlike sports, life doesn't ever play beneath its potential. It is like a good team with a killer instinct, wielding a crushing blow when its opponent is down.

You've heard the saying, "One step forward, two steps back;" in other words, for every attempt to make progress, there is a corresponding setback. This mindset leads to people settling for something less than what they really want. They reluctantly accept their position as the best underdog because they don't think being the team picked to win is even possible.

When Moses led the children of Israel out of Egypt, they arrived at the Red Sea with the Egyptian army breathing down their necks. After having second thoughts about releasing them from captivity, Pharaoh and his army pursued the Israelites with the intention of forcefully taking them back. As the Egyptian army came into view and the fear of death gripped their hearts, the Israelites began hurling accusations against Moses, blaming him for placing them in this life-threatening situation. The crisis brought Moses to his moment of truth. He had to make a decision and it had to be the right one for he wouldn't get another opportunity. This was a very serious situation.

No doubt, all of us have faced more "back against the wall" situations than we'd care to admit. One wrong decision and we'd be back under the control of a hard taskmaster. So, what should a person do during those crucial moments?

In Moses' case, he prayed to the One Who was responsible and sent him to Pharaoh, commanding that he let the Israelites go and worship. Though he turned his heart and attention to God, Moses wasn't expecting God's response.

> **And the Lord said unto Moses, Wherefore criest thou unto me? speak unto the children of Israel, that they go forward: [16]But lift thou up thy rod, and stretch out thine hand over the sea, and divide it: and the children of Israel shall go on dry ground through the midst of the sea.**
> *Exodus 14:15,16*

Remember, God commanded Moses to use the rod that was in his hand to pronounce judgment against Pharaoh and the Egyptians. He was instructed to lead the nation with that same rod. But when he realized Pharaoh and his army were on their heels, Moses started to think of himself as the underdog mentioned earlier. God had to remind him about the rod and that it was a game changer.

Moses needed God to help him change his perspective by one degree and the Red Sea was no match for them. The children of Israel passed through the Red Sea on dry land. What Moses didn't ask for was the way God fought against the Egyptian army by placing a pillar of fire in between them and closing the sea once the Egyptian army was positioned within it. This goes to prove that only one degree of change can affect situations in ways that far exceed anyone's expectations.

It's Your Time!

We have looked at examples of how athletes or an entire team gets ready for the big game. But, how does the person who isn't involved in sports get themselves in the right frame of mind to experience this level of change?

I used football only to demonstrate how an entire team can experience this principle and function collectively to accomplish a desired end. The players spent a great deal of time together preparing, training and actually playing the games. They learned how to understand their opponents together by studying films. Everything they did as a team helped them to shift their attitude so they believed victory was possible. Now it is time for you to fill your life with the proper information that causes the shift to take place in your thinking process.

It's Time to Eat

Remember, the Bible teaches that Jesus is the Word made flesh and the Word has the ability to change our entire life when we read it. The saying, "You are what you eat" is very important when it comes to reading (eating) the Word of God.

I've found that the majority of people who attend church spend very little time reading and studying the Bible. How can we be changed if we don't change the source from which we acquire information?

The human brain is very powerful and is able to produce that which a person desires. As we learn new information or principles, we develop new pathways in the brain. The more we focus on the new information, the stronger the pathways become. Since there is nothing on the earth that compares to the Word of God and its principles, the Bible is the greatest tool we can use to develop new pathways in our minds. We must begin to tap into the power of our brain if we are going to achieve our goals.

The Harvard study mentioned earlier is a powerful report about how goal setting can change a person's life. Now add the Bible to the mix and the goals we set will be turbo charged! The Word of God is alive and full of power. It is always fresh and increasing in revelation. Even if you've read a passage of Scripture dozens of times, the Word still has the ability to unveil truth you have never seen.

> **For the word of God is quick, and powerful, and sharper than any twoedged sword, piercing even to the dividing asunder of soul and spirit, and of the joints and marrow, and is a discerner of the thoughts and intents of the heart.** *Hebrews 4:12*

In the account of Moses leading the Israelites out of Egypt, God told him to look at the rod in his hand.

Many of us have a type of rod in our hands, yet we act as if we are empty handed. We cry out to God because it appears we can't go forward into our purpose and destiny and we can't go backward to the place from which we came. It is difficult for us to believe beyond the obstacle that is staring us down. But, when applied properly, the Word will open new possibilities for anyone to achieve their dreams.

The word of God infuses us with the ability to believe. We start to dream again and the faith that all things are possible comes alive. But we must become skillful in the word and understand how to use it. In the same way Moses had the rod and had used it to free the people but didn't really understand what he really had. It is the same way with many believers; they have used the word of God but haven't really tapped into its full potential.

Meditate and Grow

The Word of God will help a person achieve almost anything. Consider the following passages of Scriptures:

> **Blessed is the man that walketh not in the counsel of the ungodly, nor standeth in the way of sinners, nor sitteth in the seat of the scornful. But**

his delight is in the law of the Lord; and in his law doth he meditate day and night. *Psalm 1:1,2*

My soul shall be satisfied as with marrow and fatness; and my mouth shall praise thee with joyful lips: When I remember thee upon my bed, and meditate on thee in the night watches. *Psalm 63:5,6*

I will remember the works of the Lord: surely I will remember thy wonders of old. I will meditate also of all thy work, and talk of thy doings. *Psalm 77:11,12*

I will meditate in thy precepts, and have respect unto thy ways. I will delight myself in thy statutes: I will not forget thy word. *Psalm 119:15,16*

And I will delight myself in thy commandments, which I have loved. My hands also will I lift up unto thy commandments, which I have loved; and I will meditate in thy statutes. *Psalm 119:47,48*

I remember the days of old; I meditate on all thy works; I muse on the work of thy hands. *Psalm 143:5*

Meditate upon these things; give thyself wholly to them; that thy profiting may appear to all. Take heed unto thyself, and unto the doctrine; continue in them: for in doing this thou shalt both save thyself, and them that hear thee.
1 Timothy 4:15,16

Notice how many times the Bible instructs the believer to meditate on the Word. What we must understand about meditation is that it operates like an oven and not like a microwave. By design, a microwave cooks food very fast; a conventional oven takes much longer and requires patience to receive a finished product. During the meditation process, life gradually increases from the 211°F mark to 212°F.

When you meditate, you are programming the greatest computer ever created, the human mind. Meditation imprints what you want to do or become on the subconscious. The brain then directs the body to operate in this fashion.

A person's life will function in direct connection with their dominant thoughts! It is important to ensure that you think biblical thoughts that will help you accomplish the life goals and purpose desired. King Solomon, the richest and wisest man who ever lived, wrote two books in the

Bible, Proverbs and Ecclesiastes. It won't hurt to spend some time reading what he wrote about life and success.

Reading these books and meditating on the principles is like Solomon walking and talking with you. He is giving you the benefit of his wisdom and experiences. There may not be bells and whistles going off during your meditation but do believe that things are changing.

When I discuss meditation, there are always people who ask me what they should do differently. Most are surprised when I tell them to continue doing what they are currently doing without trying to change a thing and to start meditating on Scriptures that will help them accomplish their change. When you allow the Scriptures and meditation to change the software, everything else will have to follow suit. Before they realize it life is functioning the way the scriptures declare it will.

There are two ways a person can change the course of a ship; by taking the helm and by resetting the automatic pilot. When the automatic pilot is engaged it controls the vessel and takes it in the direction of the course set. But it can be changed by the helmsman taking hold of the helm and changing the direction. Once the helmsman relinquishes control, the ship will slowly return to its previous heading unless he disengages or recalibrates the automatic pilot. All the helmsman needs to do is change the automatic pilot settings to the new direction and the ship will stay on course. In like manner, the Word of God will reset our automatic pilot when we use it and our life will begin to follow its proper course.

Life Coach

Once you learn and put into practice this one degree principle, it will work in every area of your life. Until then, don't enter into this process alone; find someone to walk with you.

Having the right coach or mentor; that is, one who has already done what you want to do, can be of immeasurable value to the person desiring change. The coach will help you stay focused as you press through the difficulties associated with moving toward the one degree change. Even though the adjustment may pose a challenge, you must be willing to accept your coach's correction.

Many reading this book may think they can work the plan to accomplish their goals alone. If that was totally true, their lives would be changing continually and others would be

eating the fruit from their lives. DON'T LET
PRIDE KEEP YOU FROM FINDING A LIFE COACH.

Jesus used the two by two principle to send out
the disciples and it is still necessary today.

> **Two are better than one; because
> they have a good reward for their
> labour.** *Ecclesiastes 4:9*

The key to all of this is to select a coach who will
help the overall process.

A life coach should be someone outside of your
inner circle; **i.e., not** your spouse, parent, or
close friend, who is willing to oversee your
change and help you get to the next level.

The coach should be someone who understands
the Word of God and will check the Scriptures
that are being used as a source of meditation
for accuracy. Those who are unfamiliar with
meditating may feel uncomfortable at first
because their minds frequently wander into
unrelated areas. The coach will be able to help
them manage this as they go through the
infancy stages. Once the person learns how to
meditate on the Word, the process becomes
much easier and less intimidating.

The life coach will encourage dreaming and
vision casting. Since most people don't have

dreams this could be the hardest thing a coach has to do. Our football coach always painted a picture of success that made us believe we could win. The life coach must paint pictures and help the mentored do the same.

Finding a life coach can be difficult, for that reason I have a forum for further instruction and feedback. Visit BishopLarryJackson.com for more information.

Was That Real?

There is an interesting phenomenon that everyone has experienced in their lives. It is the fact that there are times when our minds can't tell the difference between reality and a dream.

People have awakened from their sleep with their hearts racing and the blood pressure elevated only to realize that what they thought was real was only a dream. It may take some time for the person to regain their composure even after they come back to reality. In fact, the dream may continue to linger in the person's mind for days. So, how does one explain this since it wasn't real; it was only a dream?

The movie industry has used this fact to draw their audience into the emotions of the movie and its characters. We call this suspension of reality 'entertainment' and Hollywood is the main benefactor.

The Mind of a Child

Have you ever watched a child come alive in their make believe world. They pretend they are slaying the fire breathing dragon, or driving a fire truck racing to put out a fire or sinking the winning basket as the buzzer sounds, or the beautiful princess at the ball? Children live this life freely, using their imaginations to create worlds to enjoy without ever leaving home. Adults even purchase toys and games that encourage their children to use their imaginations.

But once that child leaves kindergarten, they are discouraged from using their imaginations. Teachers can be heard telling students to stop day-dreaming and to come back to reality. By doing so, they are taking away one of the main ingredients associated with the one degree formula and forcing the student to settle back to 211°F or worst. The teacher could have adjusted the student by simply directing the dreams instead of discouraging them. This is one of the reasons many people don't dream today. Their teachers or some well meaning adults told them to stop dreaming and live in the real world.

Where there is no vision, the people perish: but he that keepeth the law, happy is he. *Proverbs 29:18*

[2]And the Lord answered me, and said, Write the vision, and make it plain upon tables, that he may run that readeth it. [3]For the vision is yet for an appointed time, but at the end it shall speak, and not lie: though it tarry, wait for it; because it will surely come, it will not tarry.
Habakkuk 2:2-3

Dream Producers

In this age of cable, satellite, and the Internet, so many have exchanged their personal dreams and visions for television. We have become satisfied with someone else telling us our vision (Tel-e-Vision)!

Reality television, which continues to rise in popularity, helps to build fantasy by using everyday people through whom the audience can live vicariously. Some even identify with their favorite reality star so much that they begin to mimic their hairstyle or their style of dress, their manner of speech or any other area that greatly impressed them. Essentially, their reality has become blurred and the show's vision has taken over.

Television isn't the only way visions influence our society. The video game industry has teams of people who use their imaginations to develop and later market their games to their target audience who has stopped using their imagination. We should realize that imagination and vision are still very important because those who are using their imaginations are making millions off of the people who aren't.

I recently watched a commercial that I initially thought was a movie trailer or the preview of an upcoming television program, but, to my surprise, it was a promotion for a new game that could be played on a mobile phone. Think of all of the time and money spent creating and producing this spot just to get someone to play the game. Amazing! Even more amazing is the fact that the game produces a million dollars daily.

According to venturebeat.com, Americans spent $25.3 billion on video games in 2010 and the number has continued to grow each year. While a small segment of the population profits from the use of imagination and vision, the majority of people have turned theirs off. Don't give in to this manipulation. Allow the Word of God and a seasoned coach to help you awaken your imagination again.

The Plan

Throughout this book, I have given important information about how to experience this one degree of change. Over the years, I have found that some people have difficulty pulling this type of information out of a document. They prefer a format that is more cut and dry. Every part of the plan is important and I want everyone to understand how to apply this principle in their lives and experience their one degree of change.

Here is the plan in outline form:

1. Determine what it is you want to accomplish. If you are dealing with disease, please make this your top priority. Once you are healed, move to the next priority on your list. If healing isn't a concern, start with the one thing that will help to increase and advance your life.

2. It is important to write down what success, increase or health looks like to you. Be very thorough as these definitions will help during your meditation time.

3. Select a life coach who will work with you through this process; preferably not a family member or close friend. It is important that you start to think about this person as a mentor/coach. You should schedule a weekly meeting for the first eight weeks to assess your progress.

If you have problems finding this person at first, please proceed to step three and talk it over with a spiritual leader, pastor, elder or deacon to whom you can be held accountable. This can even be your employer if they can separate your self-improvement from your work. Remember I will provide additional training and oversight as well. Visit BishopLarryJackson.com.

4. Using the concordance in your Bible to find scriptures that align with the subject area you want to accomplish. This is the "secret sauce" that brings everything to the boiling point.

Start reading and meditating on these scriptures that align with the subject area you want to accomplish. This area is the topic of discussion that you will have in sessions with the spiritual leader, pastor, elder or deacon.

For example; If you want to increase your net worth, then meditate on scriptures that teach abundance such as this scripture passage in Deuteronomy:

> **Because thou servedst not the Lord thy God with joyfulness, and with gladness of heart, for the abundance of all things;** *Deuteronomy 28:47*

In Deuteronomy 28, God explicitly tells Israel the conditions for which they can receive His blessings or His curses. This particular verse is associated with what would happen if they chose the curses instead of the blessings. If they didn't choose to serve God with joy and with a glad heart for the abundance of all things, lack and the want of all things would come on them. God is serious about the abundance of all things, not just a few things! Meditating on this fact will seal abundance of all things into the heart and soul of the person meditating.

Looking up the definition of the word you are meditating on will also help increase your understanding about the subject.

DEFINITIONS:

Abundance: An extremely plentiful or over sufficient quantity or supply: An abundance of grain

Overflowing fullness: Abundance of the heart

60

Affluence; wealth: The enjoyment of abundance

5. See yourself during these sessions the way
you want to be, or doing what you want to
accomplish. Hold that thought in your heart
as long as possible.

If your mind wonders away from the vision,
gently bring your thoughts back to center to
refocus on the vision. Never get upset at
yourself, no matter how many times your mind
wonders. Anger produces negative thoughts
and will hinder or even stop the process.

Visual Help

Now see yourself entering the bank knowing
that God loves the abundance of all things and
your bank account reflects this fact. Feel the joy
of knowing the account is full of resources and
how glad you are to know it was done by God's
hand. Remember, the mind can't tell the
difference between what's real and what's not,
but it will produce what it believes is true the
same way it does during a dream that seems
real.

6. Write everything that comes to your mind
during your times of meditation. This will be
the information to discuss with your coach
during the weekly sessions.

7. Set your heart and mind to never give up your pursuit until you realize the change you desire. This is the main ingredient for the one degree of change to take effect! Preparing for and playing the big game had more to do with attitude than anything else. It is more attitude than it is process alone.

There are people who have followed outlines like this one and still haven't experienced their change because their attitude never changed. Winning the big game was more about the team's attitude than the plays run, the uniforms, or even the opposing team. When the attitude is right, nothing else matters because the person has a single focus which changes everything.

8. Once you have accomplished the vision or goal, it is time for you to become someone's coach.

The will be the person who asks about your success and accomplishments. Just make sure they have something they want to accomplish also.

He Paid it All!

The death, burial, and resurrection of Christ provided so many benefits for us. Most are unclaimed because the body of Christ does not want to put in the work to attain them. One of the most important messages taught to the body of Christ was on the doctrine of faith. This also became a damaging teaching because many people thought everything would just be given to them. To achieve the changes we desire, we must have a mindset to apprehend what He's provided.

Listen to James:

[18]Yea, a man may say, Thou hast faith, and I have works: shew me thy faith without thy works, and I will shew thee my faith by my works. [20]But wilt thou know, O vain man, that faith without works is dead?
James 2:18, 20

The reason I believe you read this booklet is because God wants you to accomplish what He has placed in your heart. It is time for you to succeed and there is no time to waste!

Set your faith and align your heart with the Word of God. Arm yourself with a "never giving up" attitude and what seemed just out of reach will start becoming reality.

People using this principle of systematic use of the Word of God are increasing. It is now time for you to do the same. It would make my heart glad to hear about your pursuit and progress. Please feel free to contact me at info@BishopLarryJackson.com with your testimonies of advancement.

The time is now to move just one degree to experience a better life!

Remember, this will only work if you work at it! You are only one degree away from total transformation! Don't stop until you have become what you envisioned **and you are enjoying** all of the benefits that come with your change!

Summary

My aim is to teach you how to utilize the Word of God to transform your mind. The plan is relatively simple, but complex at the same time.

> **And be not conformed to this world: but be ye transformed by the renewing of your mind, that ye may prove what is that good, and**

acceptable, and perfect, will of God.
Romans 12:2

To begin this process, you must use the Scriptures in a systematic fashion three times daily during the first eight weeks. Each morning, before going to work or starting your day's activities, spend thirty minutes reading and thinking about 2 Scriptures on your list. After lunch, spend ten to fifteen minutes reading and thinking about 2 more Scriptures on your list. Finally, before retiring for bed, spend thirty minutes reading and thinking about 2 more Scriptures on your list.

If you are married, you must inform your spouse about this process. If your spouse is willing to stay the course, they can participate in the process as well. You are not a coach yet, so don't become one, not even for your spouse. If your spouse is unable to complete the process, you must press on. They may just be a fan at first, until they see your victory.

During these times, remove all distractions. Always start from the Scripture. This is not done through willpower, but through the Word of God!

Time management is very important, so use a method that will help you keep track of your progress and schedule.

Ask someone to coach you and schedule weekly meetings to report your progress. Make this easy on the person by being responsible and timely.

> **Obey them that have the rule over you, and submit yourselves: for they watch for your souls, as they that must give account, that they may do it with joy, and not with grief: for that is unprofitable for you.**
> *Hebrews 13:17*

Made in the USA
Columbia, SC
01 September 2018